this book belongs to

....

I'm very grateful to the people of Bylakuppe who welcomed us with open arms.
My thanks also to Katha, my mentors and my family.
— Malavika Navale

About Katha

Katha, a nonprofit organization founded in 1988, works in the literacy to literature continuum. We work with slum communities and municipal corporation schools to ensure that every child learns to read for fun and at grade level. We also work with women and teachers so that all children achieve their potential.

Our books, workshops and learning centres strive to forge cross-cultural connections through story and Story Pedagogy©. As one of India's finest publishers, our initiative has been recognized as "a unique and special moment in Indian publishing history," by *The Economic Times*.

Katha's books have received global recognition, including the nomination by an international jury for the prestigious Astrid Lindgren Award, the world's largest prize for children's literature.

We love to work with new and established writers, translators and illustrators.

Do you like writing, illustrating, translating for children? Write to us at kathakaar@katha.org to become a cherished member of the Katha family!

"An educational jewel in India's crown."
— Naoyuki Shinohara, Deputy Managing Director, International Monetary Fund

"Katha stands as an exemplar for all the creative projects around the world that grapple with ordinary and dramatic misery in cities." **— Charles Landry, The Art of City Making**

"Katha has a real soft corner for kids. Which is why it ... create[s] such gorgeous picture books for children."
— Time Out

"Katha's work is driven by the idea that children can bring change to their communities that is sustainable and real, just as the children do in [their books.]" **— Papertigers**

treasures from tibet

malavika navale

KATHA

Pema loved to sing, watch ants march and play hide-and-seek with her friends.

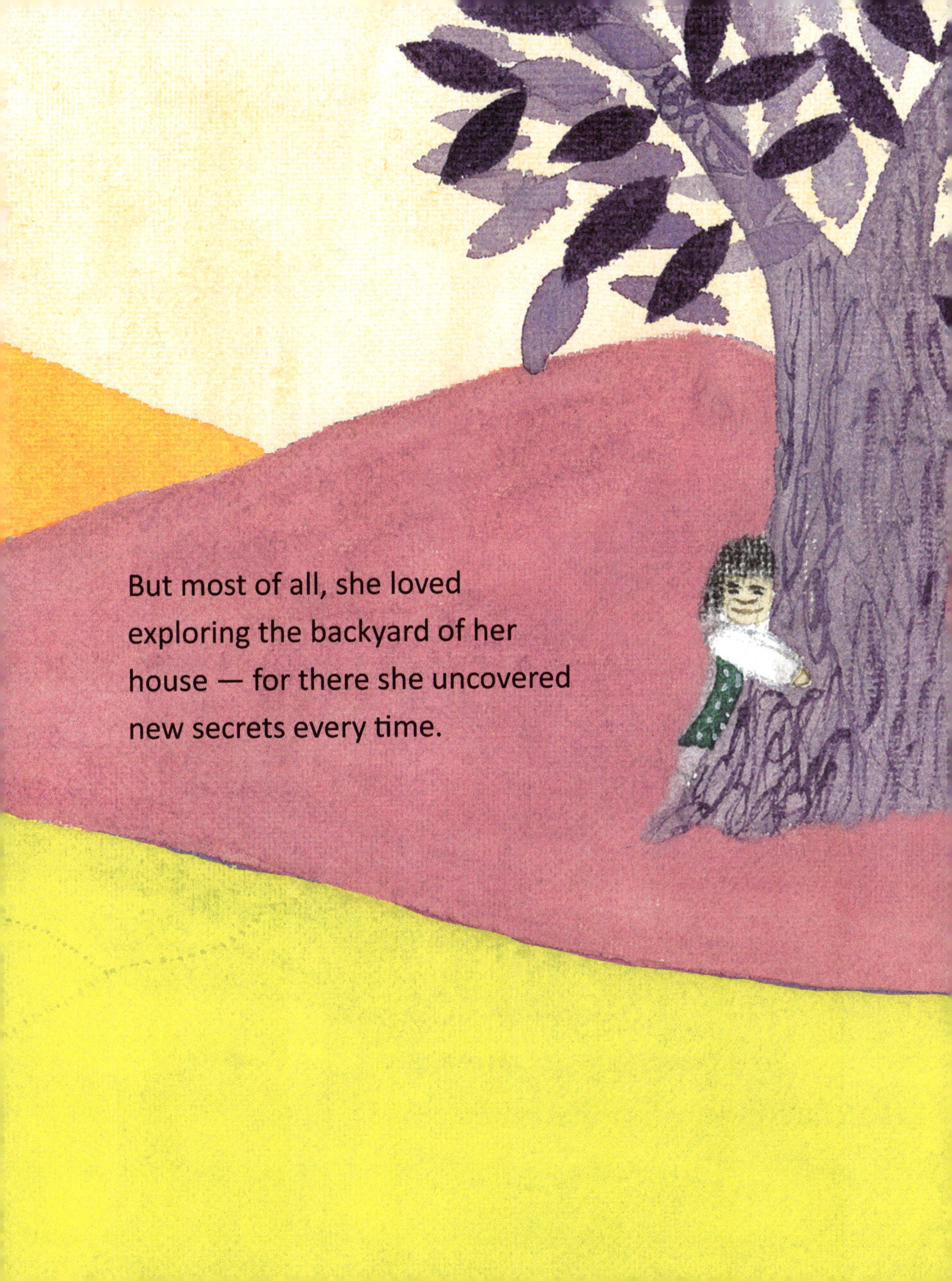

But most of all, she loved exploring the backyard of her house — for there she uncovered new secrets every time.

Her room was filled with things that she collected from the backyard. Her favourite — a butterfly wing that she spotted on the ground just the other day.

She thought the pattern on it looked exactly like the one on the floor of her house!

Late one afternoon, Pema tiptoed to her space of adventure, the backyard. Slowly but not very silently, she started to dig the ground.

She dug many holes,
holes full of nothing!

And then in the ninth hole that she dug, her hand touched something. She got to the bottom of the mystery. It was a beautiful stone!

"Eeeep!" she squealed with excitement. "I'm going to keep it with the rest of my treasure!"

She hurried back inside with her new discovery.

As Pema made her way to her room, she saw her grandmother sitting on the edge of her bed, looking at something intently.

"Momo-ley, what are you looking at?" Pema asked, stirring the stillness in the air.

"It's my treasure box, Pema," said Momo-ley. "Want to see what I keep in it?"

Pema couldn't believe that Momo-ley too had a treasure box!

"YES!" she said excitedly as she ran to Momo-ley's side.

Pema could tell that the box was very old. The edges were frayed and the joints looked worn out.

Momo-ley took out a circular metallic object which had beautiful lines carved in it.

Pema slowly traced each and every line on the coin with her finger.

She had never seen something so delicate, yet so strong.

Next, Momo-ley showed her an old black-and-white photograph. It had three women dressed beautifully in their *chubas*.

“Momo-ley, is this you?” Pema asked, pointing at the woman who stood in the middle.

“Yes!” Momo-ley smiled.

Lastly, Momo-ley very carefully took out a folded piece of paper and unwrapped it ever so gently.

"This, is my favourite treasure from Tibet," Pema's grandmother whispered into her ear.

Pema ran her fingers through the sand and held just a pinch of it.

Pema excitedly ran to her room, leaving her newest discovery from the backyard behind.

When she came back to her grandmother's room, she found her still gazing inside the box. It felt almost as if she wanted to be in it.

Pema broke the silence once more. “Momo-ley, can I show you my treasures too?”

She showed her Momo-ley a
smaller yet similar metallic object.

It was an Indian rupee.

Next, Pema showed her a
drawing she had made of herself
with her two best friends,
Chewa and Tashi.

Momo-ley said, “It’s just like the picture of me and my friends!”

Finally, Pema revealed to her a tiny box. Momo-ley opened it gently.

Momo-ley found the box to be
filled with a familiar sand —
sand from their backyard!

Momo-ley smiled. Pema smiled back happily!

The Memories of a Landscape

Tibet

Often called the Roof of the World, Tibet is in the north-east of the Himalayas. It is composed of high plateaus and some of the tallest mountains in the world. With deep valleys and snow mountains, extensive forests and grasslands, and many rivers and lakes, Tibet is one of the most beautiful places in the world.

In 1951, following a military conflict, Tibet became a part of the People's Republic of China. After which the spiritual leader of Tibet, Dalai Lama, and his followers had to seek refuge in India.

Bylakuppe

It is a tiny town in Karnataka, in the foothills of Coorg. It is the largest Tibetan settlement in South India, with a population of over 20,000 Tibetan refugees.

Momo-ley

In Tibetan, Momo-ley means 'grandmother'.

Momos

Momos are the absolutely delicious Tibetan dumplings! Wonder if they are called momos because they are usually made by Momo-leys?

Chuba

It is a traditional long-robed garment worn by the women of Tibet. If the *chuba* is worn with an apron, it signifies the woman is married.

Malavika Navale is a visual artist and a storyteller. After her early education at The Valley School, KFI, she graduated in Visual Communication from Srishti School of Art, Design and Technology, Bangalore. She's currently working as a freelance designer and illustrator, and hopes to travel the world!

Special thanks to:
Srishti School of Art, Design and Technology, especially Dr Geetha Narayanan, Meera Curam, Kavita Arvind and Srivi Kalyan, for their kind support in the making of this book.

KATHA

First published by Katha, 2015

Printed at RaveIndia, New Delhi
ISBN 978-93-82454-31-1

KATHA is a registered nonprofit organization devoted to enhancing the joys of reading amongst children and adults. Katha Schools are situated in the slums and streets of Delhi and tribal villages of Arunachal Pradesh.
A3, Sarvodaya Enclave, Sri Aurobindo Marg
New Delhi 110 017
Phone: 4141 6600 . 4182 9998 . 2652 1752
Fax: 2651 4373
E-mail: marketing@katha.org, Website: www.katha.org

Ten per cent of sales proceeds from this book will support the quality education of children studying in Katha Schools.
Katha regularly plants trees to replace the wood used in the making of its books.

Explore the idea of home with more Katha books!

A Lion in Paris

Beatrice Alemagna

Translated from the French

Join the adventures of the young, curious and lonely lion as he leaves his sunny savannah and travels to the beautiful city of Paris in search of work, love and a future.

Introduces children to the many sights of Paris, making them add one more place to their list of places to go.

The illustrations are beautiful. The concept is fantastic and so easy for even my two year old to grasp. And the idea of the lion finding fulfilment in something so simple and yet so important, is something I loved. — **Saffron Tree**

The warm and humorous story is accentuated by Alemagna's illustrations, which combine different painting techniques with collage work. — **Time Out**

A great read especially one you enjoy with your child, cuddled up next to you with a cup of cocoa. — **Parenting**

I Have a Home

Claudia Legnazzi

Translated from the Spanish

Home is where the heart is! And that's reason enough for a little girl to travel around with her mystical, magical home. From the award-winning author-illustrator Claudia Legnazzi, a book that will stay with you!

… Tugs at your imagination… — **Parenting**

www.ingramcontent.com/pod-product-compliance
Ingram Content Group UK Ltd.
Pitfield, Milton Keynes, MK11 3LW, UK
UKHW061307190726
13845UKWH00039B/1278

9 789382 454311